Quick'n'Easy
muffins and small cakes

If there is one mixture that has stood
the test of time, it has to be the simple batter we make
into a multitude of different flavoured muffins.

As muffins have increased in popularity their tastes
and textures have become more and more like small cakes.
In fact it is sometimes hard to establish if you are eating
a muffin or an individual cake.

Whatever your preference, muffins and small cakes provide
a wonderful taste adventure that can be used for anything
from a meal base to a delicious dessert.

Everything you will find in this book is for quick mixing,
saving time for the cook who likes to turn out good food
with minimum effort.

ISBN 1-74022-522-8
EAN 9781740225229
©2005 Text – Robyn Martin

R&R Publications Marketing Pty Ltd
ACN 083 612 579
PO Box 254, Carlton North, Victoria 3054, Australia
Phone: (61 3) 9381 2199   Fax: (61 3) 9381 2689
Australia wide toll-free 1800 063 296
Email: info@randrpublications.com.au
Web: www.randrpublications.com.au

Text: Robyn Martin
Photography: Alan Gillard
Typeset by Elain Wei Voon Loh
Cover photographs: (front) Very Lemon Cakes, page 48;
(back top) Muffin-Topped Chilli Con Carne, page 44, and
Asparagus Slice with Crisp Prosciutto and Hollandaise Sauce, page 44;
(back bottom) Minted Pea Muffins, page 10
Crockery supplied by Country Road
Recipes tested by Virginia Hewin and Rosemary Hurdley
Proofreader: Gabrielle Wilson
Printed in Singapore

WEIGHTS AND MEASURES
All recipes in this book have been tested using standard metric
measuring cups and spoons. All cup and spoon measures are level
and brown sugar measures are firmly packed. Standard-sized eggs
are used.

contents

savoury muffins   7

sweet muffins   21

muffin mixtures   35

small cakes   47

index   64

TIPS FOR MAKING PERFECT MUFFINS AND SMALL CAKES

MIXING MUFFINS

It is important to mix muffins quickly until the ingredients are just wet. Muffins peak up like erupting volcanoes, become tough to eat and have a lot of tunnels in them if they are over-mixed. Use a fork.

REMOVING MUFFINS FROM PANS

Muffins can usually be easily removed from the pans by placing a folded tea towel or clean cloth over them when they come out of the oven. Leave to cool with the cloth over them for about 10 minutes before removing muffins from the pan.

COOKING TIMES FOR VARIOUS MUFFIN PANS

Different-sized muffin pans are available. Any muffin mixture can be cooked in any sized pan depending on how you want to serve the muffins. Use these cooking times as a guide. Muffins are cooked when they spring back when lightly touched. Cook at 190°C–200°C.

- Mini muffins for 10–15 minutes
- Regular deep muffins for 15–20 minutes
- Jumbo muffins or Texas muffins for 20–25 minutes

SUBSTITUTE INGREDIENTS

Substitute a mixture of ¾ soy milk and ¼ water for milk
to make dairy-free muffins.

Substitute dairy-free margarine, olive oil or olive-oil spread
for butter in any muffin recipe. Make sure you read the
ingredients in the margarine or olive-oil spread as many
brands have milk powder added.

COOKING TIMES FOR BIG CAKES MADE USING SMALL CAKE MIXTURES

Regular mixtures in a 20cm round cake tin will usually
bake at 180°C for 45–60 minutes. Fruit cake mixtures may
take longer.

CAKE TINS

There are a whole host of different cake tins available for
small cakes. Cooking time will vary depending on the
depth of the tin. If you are unable to buy friand tins from
your local kitchen store, try the Internet. There are plenty
of kitchen-equipment websites.

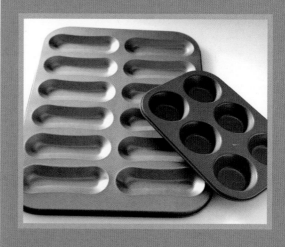

savoury muffins

Who needs bread when you can russle up a quick

batch of muffins to fill for lunch, serve with soup

or use as a meal base.

Whatever your needs, take a basic muffin mixture and

add whatever savoury flavours you like to create

your own savoury muffin special.

Savoury muffins have no sugar so tend to be paler than

their sweet counterparts.

Dill and Horseradish Muffins with Smoked Salmon Makes 10.

See photograph on pages 6–7.

2 cups plain flour

3 teaspoons baking powder

$^1/_4$ teaspoon salt

2 tablespoons chopped fresh dill

$^1/_4$ cup horseradish cream

1 egg

$1^1/_4$ cups milk

cream cheese

smoked salmon

fresh dill to garnish

Sift flour, baking powder and salt into a bowl. Make a well in the centre of the dry ingredients. Mix dill, horseradish and egg together until combined. Add to dry ingredients with milk and mix until just combined. Fill greased deep muffin pans with mixture. Bake at 190°C for 15 minutes or until muffins spring back when lightly touched. Serve fresh spread with cream cheese and topped with smoked salmon. Garnish with a sprig of fresh dill.

Lemon and Thyme Muffins Makes 8. See photograph on page 9.

2 cups plain flour

3 teaspoons baking powder

$^1/_4$ teaspoon salt

50g butter

2 teaspoons grated lemon rind

2 teaspoons dried thyme

$^1/_4$ cup lemon juice

1 egg

1 cup milk

Sift flour, baking powder and salt into a bowl. Make a well in the centre of the dry ingredients. Melt butter. Mix in lemon rind, thyme and lemon juice. Lightly beat egg. Pour butter mixture, egg and milk into dry ingredients and mix until just combined. Fill greased deep muffin pans with mixture. Bake at 180°C for 15–20 minutes or until muffins spring back when lightly touched. Serve warm with a casserole or roast chicken.

Fresh Herb Muffins Makes 28 mini muffins or 10 regular muffins. (Not photographed.)

2 cups plain flour

3 teaspoons baking powder

$^1/_4$ teaspoon salt

$1^1/_2$ cups chopped mixed fresh herbs such as parsley, chives and dill in any proportions

2 eggs

2 tablespoons oil

1 cup milk

Sift flour, baking powder and salt into a bowl. Mix through herbs. Make a well in the centre of the dry ingredients. Beat eggs, oil and milk together. Pour milk mixture into dry ingredients and mix to just moisten Three-quarters fill greased mini-muffin pans or regular muffin pans with mixture. Bake at 200°C for 10 minutes for mini muffins or 15 minutes for regular muffins or until muffins spring back when lightly touched. Serve with butter as a snack.

Minted Pea Muffins Makes 10.

1 cup frozen minted peas
1¼ cups chicken stock
2 cups plain flour
4 teaspoons baking powder
¼ teaspoon salt
2 eggs
2 tablespoons olive oil
½ cup milk

Cook peas in stock for 7 minutes. Cool, then mash in the cooking liquid using a potato masher. Sift flour, baking powder and salt into a bowl. Make a well in the centre of the dry ingredients. Beat eggs, oil and milk together until combined. Pour egg and pea mixtures into the well. Mix quickly until just combined. Fill greased deep muffin pans with mixture. Bake at 190°C for 10–15 minutes or until muffins spring back when lightly touched. For a winter taste treat, serve with homemade pea and ham soup.

Cheese Muffins Makes 10.

2 cups plain flour

4 teaspoons baking powder

$^1/_2$ teaspoon hot smoked paprika

1 cup grated tasty cheese

1 egg

1$^1/_4$ cups milk

120g feta cheese

Sift flour, baking powder and paprika into a bowl. Mix in tasty cheese. Make a well in the centre of the dry ingredients. Lightly beat egg. Mix into milk. Pour into dry ingredients and mix until just combined. Fill greased deep muffin pans with mixture. Crumble feta over top of muffins. Bake at 180°C for 15–20 minutes or until muffins spring back when lightly touched.

Roasted Capsicum Muffins Makes 8. See photograph on page 13.

2 medium red capsicums
2 cups plain flour
4 teaspoons baking powder
$1/2$ teaspoon salt
1 egg
2 tablespoons olive oil
2 teaspoons prepared, crushed chilli
1 cup milk

Cut capsicums in half. Remove seeds and core and place cut side down on a baking tray. Grill until skins are blistered. Remove skins when cool enough to handle. Cut capsicum halves in half again. Use a capsicum quarter to partly line the base and sides of greased deep muffin pans. Sift flour, baking powder and salt into a bowl. Make a well in the centre of the dry ingredients. Lightly beat egg, oil and chilli together. Pour into dry ingredients with milk and mix quickly until just combined. Spoon mixture into capsicum-lined muffin pans to three-quarters fill. Bake at 190°C for 15 minutes or until muffins spring back when lightly touched. Serve upside down, split and filled with chilli jam or red capsicum relish.

Walnut and Blue Cheese Muffins Makes 30 mini muffins or about 12 regular muffins.
(Not photographed.)

100g blue vein cheese
$1/2$ cup chopped walnuts
2 cups plain flour
4 teaspoons baking powder
1 tablespoon sugar
2 eggs
1 cup milk

Crumble blue vein cheese into a bowl large enough to mix muffins in. Add walnuts and mix. Sift flour and baking powder into bowl. Stir in sugar. Make a well in the centre of the dry ingredients. Beat eggs and milk together. Pour into dry ingredients. Mix to just moisten. Three-quarters fill greased mini-muffin pans or regular muffin pans with mixture. Bake at 190°C for 10–15 minutes for mini muffins or 20 minutes for regular muffins or until muffins spring back when lightly touched. Serve with sliced fresh pear.

WALNUT, PEAR AND BLUE CHEESE MUFFINS
Replace milk with unsweetened pear juice and add 1 cup chopped canned pears with egg mixture.

Tomato and Chorizo Muffins Makes 8.

2 cups plain flour
4 teaspoons baking powder
$^1/_2$ teaspoon salt
1 egg
2 tablespoons olive oil
2 chorizo sausages
1$^1/_4$ cups milk
4 cherry tomatoes
shaved Parmesan cheese

Sift flour, baking powder and salt into a bowl. Make a well in the centre of the dry ingredients. Lightly beat egg and oil together until combined. Cut sausages into 1cm pieces. Mix sausages, egg mixture and milk into dry ingredients until just combined. Fill greased deep muffin pans with mixture. Cut tomatoes in half crosswise. Place half a tomato on top of mixture cut-side up. Bake at 190°C for 15 minutes or until muffins are cooked. Remove from oven and place a thin shaving of Parmesan cheese over the top of each muffin.

Carrot and Coriander Muffins Makes 12.

2 cups plain flour

4 teaspoons baking powder

$^1/_4$ teaspoon salt

$1^1/_2$ cups grated carrot

$^1/_4$ cup chopped fresh coriander

$^1/_2$ cup sherry

2 eggs

$^3/_4$ cup milk

Sift flour, baking powder and salt into a bowl. Make a well in the centre of the dry ingredients. Mix carrot, coriander, sherry and eggs together until combined. Add carrot mixture and milk to dry ingredients and mix until just combined. Fill greased deep muffin pans with mixture. Bake at 190°C for 15–20 minutes or until muffins spring back when lightly touched.

Apple and Sausage Muffins Makes 4. See photograph on page 17.

Soft breadcrumbs are made from stale bread. They are not toasted.

4 pork sausages

2 apples

1¹/₂ cups soft breadcrumbs

¹/₂ cup rolled oats

2 eggs

TOASTED CROUTON

4 slices toast bread

1 clove garlic

2 tablespoons olive oil

Remove casing from sausages and place sausage meat in a bowl. Wash apples. Cut into quarters and remove cores. Cut two quarters into six slices each. Chop remaining apple roughly, leaving skin on. Add chopped apple to sausage meat with breadcrumbs, rolled oats and eggs. Mix with clean hands until combined. Fill jumbo muffin pans with mixture. Push three apple slices into each muffin. Bake at 190°C for 25–30 minutes or until cooked. Serve hot on a toasted crouton with salad greens and relish.

TOASTED CROUTON

Cut four, 8cm rounds from each bread slice. Crush and peel the garlic. Brush bread with oil on both sides. Rub garlic clove over oiled bread. Bake at 190°C for 10 minutes or until crisp and golden.

Olive and Feta Muffins Makes 30 mini muffins or about 12 regular muffins. (Not photographed.)

2 cups plain flour

3 teaspoons baking powder

50g butter

1 egg

100g feta cheese

1 cup milk

1 cup chopped, pitted black olives

1 teaspoon dried rosemary

Sift flour and baking powder into a bowl. Make a well in the centre of the dry ingredients. Melt butter. Beat in egg. Cut cheese into 1cm cubes. Add butter mixture, milk, cheese, olives and rosemary to dry ingredients. Mix until just combined. Three-quarters fill greased mini-muffin pans or regular muffin pans with mixture. Bake at 190°C for 10–15 minutes for mini muffins or 20–25 minutes for regular muffins or until muffins spring back when lightly touched. Serve warm, split and filled with cheese or pastrami.

French Onion Muffins Makes 10. (Not photographed.)

2 medium onions

2 tablespoons oil

50g butter

2 cups plain flour

4 teaspoons baking powder

¹/₂ teaspoon salt

2 eggs

1 cup milk

1 cup grated Gruyère cheese

Peel onions and cut into thin rings. Heat oil in a frying pan and fry onions over medium heat until golden. Add butter to pan and melt. Remove from heat and set aside. Sift flour, baking powder and salt into a bowl. Make a well in the centre of the dry ingredients. Lightly beat eggs and milk. Add onion and egg mixtures to dry ingredients. Mix quickly until just combined. Three-quarters fill greased muffin pans with mixture. Sprinkle with grated cheese. Bake at 200°C for 15 minutes or until muffins spring back when lightly touched. Serve as a snack.

Thai Muffins Makes 10.

2 kaffir lime leaves

2 cups plain flour

3 teaspoons baking powder

2 eggs

165g jar Thai flavour base

1/4 cup chopped fresh coriander

1 cup coconut milk

Cut mid rib from centre of lime leaves. Shred leaves very finely. Sift flour and baking powder into a bowl and mix through shredded lime leaves. Make a well in the centre of the dry ingredients. Lightly beat eggs. Mix eggs, Thai flavour base, coriander and coconut milk together. Pour into dry ingredients and mix until just combined. Fill greased deep muffin pans with mixture. Bake at 180°C for 15–20 minutes or until muffins spring back when lightly touched. Serve with pumpkin soup.

Moroccan Muffins Makes 14.

1 cup couscous

1 cup boiling water

1 onion

2 tablespoons oil

2 teaspoons ground cumin

2 teaspoons ground coriander

1$^1/_2$ cups plain flour

4 teaspoons baking powder

$^1/_2$ teaspoon salt

2 eggs

1$^1/_2$ cups milk

$^1/_2$ cup raisins

Place couscous in a bowl. Pour boiling water over and set aside. Peel onion and chop finely. Heat oil in a frying pan and sauté onion for 5 minutes or until clear not coloured. Add cumin and coriander and cook over a low heat until spices smell fragrant. Sift flour, baking powder and salt into a bowl. Make a well in the centre of the dry ingredients. Lightly beat eggs. Add eggs, milk, raisins and onion mixture to dry ingredients and mix quickly until just combined. Fill greased deep muffin pans with mixture. Bake at 190°C for 15–20 minutes or until muffins spring back when lightly touched. Serve warm with cold chicken and Moroccan relish.

sweet muffins

There are few eating occasions where a sweet
muffin doesn't fit.

For morning or afternoon tea, in a lunch box
or for a sweet treat at the end of a meal,
sweet muffins are a simple and versatile goodie to have
in your repertoire of cooking skills and recipe ideas.

Chocolate Brownie Muffins with Mixed Berry Sauce Makes 10. See photograph on pages 20–21.

250g butter

$^1/_2$ cup cocoa

100g dark chocolate

$1^1/_4$ cups sugar

4 eggs

2 teaspoons vanilla essence

$1^1/_4$ cups plain flour

1 teaspoon baking powder

MIXED BERRY SAUCE

1 cup frozen mixed berries

$^1/_2$ cup mixed berry jam

$^1/_2$ cup ready-made chocolate sauce

Place butter, cocoa and chocolate in a saucepan large enough to mix all the ingredients. Melt over a medium heat. Stir in sugar. Allow to cool. Beat in eggs and vanilla. Sift over flour and baking powder and combine well. Three-quarters fill paper muffin cups with mixture. Bake at 180°C for 12 minutes. Serve muffins warm with warm berry sauce and cream.

MIXED BERRY SAUCE

Thaw berries and mash lightly. Place in a saucepan with jam. Heat until jam melts and berries are hot. Remove from heat and stir in chocolate sauce.

Prune and Orange Muffins Makes 10. See photograph on page 23.

The packet says dried plums; that's just another name for prunes.

$1^1/_2$ cups chopped orange-flavoured dried plums

$^1/_4$ cup brown sugar

1 cup orange juice

50g butter

2 eggs

2 cups plain flour

3 teaspoons baking powder

Place plums, brown sugar, orange juice and butter in a saucepan large enough to mix all the ingredients. Heat gently until butter melts. Remove from heat and cool. Beat eggs into plum mixture with a wooden spoon. Sift in flour and baking powder and mix until just combined. Three-quarters fill deep greased muffin pans with mixture. Bake at 190°C for 15 minutes or until muffins spring back when lightly touched.

Carrot and Honey Muffins Makes 14. (Not photographed.)

2 cups plain flour

2 teaspoons bicarbonate of soda

1 teaspoon mixed spice

$^1/_2$ cup raw sugar

$^1/_2$ cup honey

$2^1/_2$ cups grated carrot

$^1/_2$ cup raisins

3 eggs

1 cup oil

Sift flour, baking soda and mixed spice into a bowl. Stir in raw sugar. Make a well in the centre of the dry ingredients. Pour honey into dry ingredients. Add carrot and raisins. Beat eggs and oil together. Add to mixing bowl. Mix to just moisten. Three-quarters fill greased deep muffin pans. Bake at 200°C for 20 minutes or until muffins spring back when lightly touched. Serve warm or cold.

Bran and Sticky Raisin Muffins Makes 12.

1 cup wholemeal flour

1 teaspoon baking powder

$^1/_2$ teaspoon salt

$1^1/_2$ cups baking bran

$^1/_4$ cup sugar

1 cup sticky raisins

50g butter

2 tablespoons golden syrup

1 egg

$1^1/_4$ cups milk

1 teaspoon bicarbonate of soda

Mix flour, baking powder, salt, bran, sugar and raisins together in a bowl. Make a well in the centre of the dry ingredients. Melt butter and golden syrup together. Lightly beat egg. Mix milk and bicarbonate of soda together. Pour butter mixture, egg and milk into dry ingredients and mix until just combined. Three-quarters fill greased deep muffin pans with mixture. Bake at 200°C for 15–20 minutes or until muffins spring back when lightly touched.

Raspberry and Rhubarb Muffins Makes 10.

$^1/_2$ **cup fresh or thawed frozen raspberries**

$^1/_2$ **cup cooked rhubarb**

$^1/_4$ **cup sugar**

2 cups plain flour

4 teaspoons baking powder

1 teaspoon mixed spice

1 egg

50g butter

$^3/_4$ **cup milk**

icing sugar

Mix raspberries, rhubarb and sugar together. Sift flour, baking powder and mixed spice into a bowl. Make a well in the centre of the dry ingredients. Lightly beat egg. Melt butter. Pour rhubarb mixture, egg, butter and milk into dry ingredients. Mix until just combined. Three-quarters fill paper muffin cups with mixture. Bake at 200°C for 15–20 minutes or until muffins spring back when lightly touched. Serve warm, dusted with icing sugar.

Date and Marsala Muffins Makes 10.

2 cups pitted dates

$^1/_2$ cup brown sugar

$^1/_2$ cup marsala

2 cups plain flour

3 teaspoons baking powder

1 teaspoon mixed spice

$^1/_4$ cup brown sugar

2 eggs

1$^1/_4$ cups milk

Chop dates roughly. Place dates, first measure of brown sugar and marsala in a saucepan. Bring to the boil and simmer for 5 minutes. Cool. Sift flour, baking powder and mixed spice into a bowl. Mix in second measure of brown sugar. Make a well in the centre of the dry ingredients. Lightly beat eggs. Pour eggs and milk into dry ingredients and mix to just combine. Spoon two tablespoons of date mixture into the base of paper muffin cups. Place in deep muffin pans. Three-quarters fill with muffin mixture. Bake at 190°C for 12–15 minutes or until muffins spring back when lightly touched. To serve, turn muffins upside down. Cut a cross in the base of the paper cups. Peel cups open to reveal date mixture.

Chocolate Spice Muffins Makes 10.

2 cups plain flour

$^1/_4$ cup cocoa

3 teaspoons baking powder

$1^1/_2$ teaspoons ground cinnamon

$^1/_4$ cup sugar

2 eggs

2 teaspoons vanilla essence

50g butter

$1^1/_4$ cups milk

Sift flour, cocoa, baking powder and cinnamon into a bowl. Stir in sugar. Make a well in the centre of the dry ingredients. Lightly beat eggs and vanilla together. Melt butter. Mix eggs, butter and milk together and pour into dry ingredients. Mix quickly until just combined. Three-quarters fill greased deep muffin pans with mixture. Bake at 200°C for 15–20 minutes or until muffins spring back when lightly touched.

Cherry Muffins Makes 12.

2 cups plain flour

3 teaspoons baking powder

$^1/_4$ cup sugar

50g butter

1 egg

1 cup buttermilk

1 teaspoon almond essence

425g can drained pitted black cherries

Sift flour and baking powder into a bowl. Mix in sugar. Make a well in the centre of the dry ingredients. Melt butter. Lightly beat egg. Mix buttermilk and almond essence together. Pour butter, egg, buttermilk and cherries into dry ingredients. Mix quickly until just combined. Three-quarters fill greased deep muffin pans with mixture. Bake at 190°C for 15–20 minutes or until muffins spring back when lightly touched.

Honey and Hazelnut Muffins Makes 24 mini muffins or 12 regular muffins.

If you want to make regular deep muffins with this mixture, use $^1/_2$ cup honey and $^1/_2$ cup chopped hazelnuts for the topping.

2 cups plain flour

1 teaspoon baking soda

1 teaspoon baking powder

$^1/_2$ cup bran

$^1/_2$ cup finely chopped roasted hazelnuts

1 egg

$^1/_2$ cup liquid honey

1 cup milk

$^1/_4$ cup honey

$^1/_4$ cup coarsely chopped hazelnuts

Sift flour, baking powder and baking soda into a bowl. Mix in bran and first measure of hazelnuts. Make a well in the centre of the dry ingredients. Lightly beat egg and $^1/_4$ **cup** of the honey together. Pour into dry ingredients with milk. Mix until just combined. Three-quarters fill greased mini-muffin pans with the mixture. Mix remaining honey and second measure of hazelnuts together. Spoon a tablespoon of hazelnut mixture over muffin mixture. Bake at 190°C for 10–15 minutes or until muffins spring back when lightly touched.

Peach Melba Muffins Makes 10.

2 cups plain flour

4 teaspoons baking powder

$^1/_4$ cup sugar

410g can peaches in natural juice

50g butter

1 egg

$^1/_2$ cup reserved peach juice

$^1/_2$ cup milk

$^1/_2$ cup raspberry jam

Sift flour and baking powder into a bowl. Mix in sugar. Make a well in the centre of the dry ingredients. Drain peaches reserving $^1/_2$ cup juice. Cut peaches into 0.5cm cubes. Melt butter. Lightly beat egg. Mix butter, egg, reserved peach juice and milk together. Pour into dry ingredients and mix until just combined. Half fill greased deep muffin pans with mixture. Spoon 2 teaspoons of raspberry jam into centre of mixture. Top with muffin mixture to three-quarters fill muffin pans. Bake at 180°C for 15–20 minutes or until muffins spring back when lightly touched.

Bread and Butter Muffins Makes 10.

5 slices stale bread

¹/₂ cup raspberry jam

1 cup plain flour

1 teaspoon baking powder

¹/₄ cup sugar

3 eggs

2 teaspoons vanilla essence

50g butter

¹/₂ cup milk

fresh berries

softly whipped cream

Cut crusts from bread. Spread slices with raspberry jam and cut into 2cm cubes. Half fill deep greased muffin pans with bread cubes. Sift flour and baking powder into a bowl. Mix in sugar. Make a well in the centre of the dry ingredients. Lightly beat eggs and vanilla together. Melt butter. Pour eggs, butter and milk into dry ingredients and mix until just combined. Pour mixture over bread cubes to almost fill muffin pans. Bake at 190°C for 15 minutes or until muffins are firm. Serve warm with berries and softly whipped cream.

Apple Dumpling Muffins
Makes 8. See photograph on page 33 (top).

1 Granny Smith apple

2 cups plain flour

3 teaspoons baking powder

1/2 teaspoon ground cloves

1/4 cup brown sugar

50g butter

2 eggs

1 cup milk

1/4 cup golden syrup

Peel apple and cut into quarters. Cut quarters into wedges. Sift flour, baking powder and cloves into a bowl. Mix in brown sugar. Make a well in the centre of the dry ingredients. Melt butter. Lightly beat eggs. Pour butter, eggs and milk into dry ingredients and mix until just combined. Half fill greased deep muffin pans with mixture. Dip each apple piece into golden syrup to cover. Press into the centre of the muffin mixture. Top with remaining muffin mixture to fill muffin pans. Push wedges of apple into the top of each muffin. Bake at 190°C for 15–20 minutes or until muffin mixture is firm. Serve with fresh cream.

Crushed Berry and White Chocolate Muffins
Makes 12. See photograph on page 33 (bottom).

2 cups plain flour

3 teaspoons baking powder

1/4 cup sugar

1/2 cup white chocolate melts

2 eggs

1 cup milk

2 cups fresh or thawed frozen boysenberries or blueberries

Sift flour and baking powder into a bowl. Mix in sugar. Make a well in the centre of the dry ingredients. Melt chocolate melts to packet directions. Lightly beat eggs. Pour eggs, milk and chocolate into dry ingredients. Lightly crush berries with a potato masher. Add to mixture and mix until just combined and ripple-like. Three-quarters fill greased deep muffin pans with mixture. Bake at 190°C for 15–20 minutes or until muffins spring back when lightly touched.

Rhubarb and Lemon Muffins
Makes 14. (Not photographed.)

1 cup stewed rhubarb

2 teaspoons grated lemon rind

2 cups plain flour

4 teaspoons baking powder

3/4 cup sugar

50g butter

2 eggs

1 cup milk

Mix rhubarb and lemon rind together. Sift flour and baking powder into a bowl. Stir in sugar. Make a well in the centre of the dry ingredients. Melt butter. Beat eggs and milk together. Mix rhubarb, milk mixture and butter into dry ingredients to just moisten. Three-quarters fill greased muffin pans. Bake at 200°C for 15 minutes or until muffins spring back when lightly touched.

muffin mixtures

Who said you had to cook your muffin mixture in a muffin pan?
No-one of course! When quick, delicious meals are
what you need, look outside the square and
be creative – just like we have done here.

Beetroot, Feta and Pistachio Muffin Slice Serves 6. See photograph on pages 34–35.

450g can baby beetroot

2 cups plain flour

4 teaspoons baking powder

$^1/_2$ teaspoon salt

$^1/_2$ cup chopped fresh chives or
spring onion greens

2 eggs

2 tablespoons olive oil

$1^1/_4$ cups milk

100g feta cheese

$^1/_2$ cup shelled, chopped pistachio nuts

Drain beetroot. Cut beetroot in half lengthwise. Sift flour, baking powder and salt into a bowl. Mix in chives or spring onion greens. Make a well in the centre of the dry ingredients. Beat eggs and oil together until combined. Pour into dry ingredients with milk and mix quickly until just combined. Line the base of a 20 x 30cm sponge roll tin with baking paper. Spread mixture into the tin. Arrange beetroot over the mixture, cut-side down. Crumble over feta and sprinkle pistachio nuts over the top. Bake at 190°C for 30 minutes or until mixture is cooked. Serve cut into slices.

Breakfast Egg Muffins Serves 4. see photograph on page 37.

2 cups plain flour

3 teaspoons baking powder

$^1/_2$ teaspoon salt

50g butter

5 eggs

1 cup milk

$^1/_2$ cup chopped mixed fresh herbs such
as parsley, chives and dill

100g feta cheese

grilled bacon

maple syrup

tomato relish

Sift flour, baking powder and salt into a bowl. Make a well in the centre of the dry ingredients. Melt butter. Lightly beat one egg. Pour butter, egg, milk and herbs into dry ingredients and mix quickly until just combined. Line the base of a 23cm square slice tin with baking paper. Spread mixture into the tin. Make four indentations in the surface of the mixture and break an egg into each indentation. Crumble over feta. Bake at 190°C for 15 minutes or until eggs are set and muffin mixture cooked. Cut into squares allowing one egg per serving. Serve hot with grilled bacon and maple syrup or tomato relish.

Curried Chicken Muffin Bake Serves 6.

850g boneless chicken pieces

80g sachet green curry paste

2 cups plain flour

4 teaspoons baking powder

$1/4$ teaspoon salt

2 eggs

1 cup coconut milk

3 bananas

1 tablespoon oil

chopped fresh coriander
or parsley to garnish

Trim any fat from chicken. Cut chicken into bite-sized pieces. Reserve one tablespoon of curry paste. Mix chicken with remaining curry paste. Place into a 25cm square ovenproof dish. Sift flour, baking powder and salt into a bowl. Make a well in the centre of the dry ingredients. Beat eggs and reserved curry paste together until combined. Pour into dry ingredients with coconut milk. Mix quickly until just combined. Spread mixture over chicken. Peel bananas and cut in half lengthwise. Arrange cut-side up over muffin mixture. Brush with oil. Bake at 180°C for 30–35 minutes or until chicken is cooked and muffin mixture springs back when lightly touched. Serve garnished with chopped coriander or parsley.

Rosemary and Onion-Jam Muffin Loaf Serves 6.

Make your own onion jam or buy it ready-made.

2 cups plain flour

4 teaspoons baking powder

$^1/_4$ teaspoon salt

2 eggs

2 tablespoons wholegrain mustard

2 tablespoons olive oil

$1^1/_4$ cups milk

1 cup onion jam

1 tablespoon rosemary leaves

Sift flour, baking powder and salt into a bowl. Make a well in the centre of the dry ingredients. Beat eggs and mustard together until combined. Mix oil and milk into egg mixture. Pour into dry ingredients and mix quickly until just combined. Line the base of 22 x12cm loaf tin with baking paper. Spoon half the mixture into the tin. Spread onion jam down the centre of the mixture. Sprinkle over half the rosemary leaves. Top with remaining mixture and rosemary leaves. Bake at 180°C for 40 minutes or until the loaf springs back when lightly touched. Serve warm, cut into slices.

Magic Muffins Makes 8.

Top these with whatever you like.

2 cups plain flour

4 teaspoons baking powder

$^1/_4$ teaspoon salt

1 teaspoon dried thyme

50g butter

2 eggs

1 cup milk

6 rashers bacon

Sift flour, baking powder and salt into a bowl. Mix in thyme. Make a well in the centre of the dry ingredients. Melt butter. Lightly beat eggs. Pour butter, eggs and milk into dry ingredients. Mix to combine. Heat an electric frying pan, griddle or flat-based frying pan. Oil pan. Place 10cm poaching rings in pan and pour muffin mixture to half fill rings. Cook over a medium to hot heat for 4 minutes or until golden. Turn and cook other side for 4 minutes. Grill bacon. Serve topped with mushroom topping and bacon.

MUSHROOM TOPPING

300g brown button mushrooms

1 small onion

1 clove garlic

25g butter

2 tablespoons oil

2 tablespoons plain flour

1 cup vegetable stock

2 tablespoons marsala

2 tablespoons chopped fresh parsley

MUSHROOM TOPPING

Clean and trim mushrooms, cutting in half if mushrooms are too big. Peel onion and chop finely. Crush garlic and chop finely. Melt butter and oil in pan and sauté onion and garlic for 3 minutes. Add mushrooms and sauté for 3 minutes. Add flour and cook to combine. Remove from heat and mix in stock and marsala. Cook, stirring until mixture boils and thickens. Stir in parsley.

COOK'S TIP

Mix the base of this magic muffin recipe and top with smoked salmon mixed with sour cream, horseradish cream and chopped fresh dill. Garnish with chopped roasted walnuts – delicious.

Quince Paste, Blue Cheese and Walnut Fingers Makes about 12 fingers.

Use a strong cheddar for these fingers if blue cheese isn't your taste. Serve these fingers with a cheese and fruit selection for lunch or as an alternative to dessert after dinner.

2 cups plain flour
4 teaspoons baking powder
2 tablespoons sugar
2 eggs
2 tablespoons olive oil
1 cup milk
120g quince paste
140g blue cheese
26 walnut pieces

Sift flour and baking powder into a bowl. Mix in sugar. Make a well in the centre of the dry ingredients. Lightly beat the eggs and oil together to combine. Pour egg mixture and milk into dry ingredients and mix quickly to just combine. Line the base of a 20 x 30cm sponge roll tin with baking paper. Pour mixture into the tin. Slice quince paste finely. Arrange paste in rows about 1.5cm apart over muffin mixture. Crumble over blue cheese and arrange a walnut piece on each quince paste slice. Bake at 180°C for 15–20 minutes or until mixture springs back when lightly touched. Serve cut into fingers.

Apple Strudel Muffin Dessert Serves 4–6.

If cooking this in a shallow dish 20–25 minutes cooking time should be allowed.

567g can spiced apples

$^1/_2$ cup sultanas

1$^1/_2$ cups plain flour

2 teaspoons baking powder

$^3/_4$ cup rolled oats

2 eggs

$^1/_2$ cup brown sugar

50g butter

1 cup milk

$^1/_2$ cup chopped pecans

Place apples in a five-cup capacity ovenproof dish. Mix through sultanas. Sift flour and baking powder into a bowl. Mix in oats. Make a well in the centre of the dry ingredients. Lightly beat eggs and sugar together until combined. Melt butter. Mix egg mixture, butter and milk into dry ingredients until just combined. Pour over apples, spreading to cover. Sprinkle with pecans. Bake at 190°C for 30–35 minutes or until topping springs back when lightly touched. Serve hot with cream or ice cream.

Muffin-Topped Chilli Con Carne Makes 5.

350g lean beef mince
425g can chilli beans
290g can tomato puree
2 cups plain flour
4 teaspoons baking powder
$1/2$ teaspoon salt
$1/2$ cup fine cornmeal
2 eggs
410g can cream-style sweetcorn
1 cup milk
1 cup grated tasty cheese

Brown mince in a saucepan. Remove from heat. Add chilli beans and tomato puree. Divide mixture among five individual one-cup capacity ramekins. Sift flour, baking powder and salt into a bowl. Mix in cornmeal. Make a well in the centre of the dry ingredients. Lightly beat eggs. Mix into sweetcorn. Add to dry ingredients with milk. Mix quickly until just combined. Spoon mixture over mince. Sprinkle with cheese. Bake at 200°C for 20–25 minutes or until muffin mixture springs back when lightly touched. Serve with avocado or tomato salsa.

Asparagus Slice with Crisp Prosciutto and Hollandaise Sauce Serves 8.

Aioli makes a good alternative to hollandaise sauce if wished. Make your own hollandaise sauce or use a ready-made variety.

2 cups plain flour
4 teaspoons baking powder
$1/4$ teaspoon salt
$1/2$ teaspoon mustard powder
$1^1/2$ cups grated tasty cheese
2 eggs
$1^1/4$ cups milk
11 spears asparagus
6 slices prosciutto
1 cup hollandaise sauce

Sift flour, baking powder, salt and mustard into a bowl. Mix through cheese. Make a well in the centre of the dry ingredients. Lightly beat eggs. Mix into milk. Pour milk mixture into dry ingredients and mix quickly until just combined. Line the base of a 22cm cake tin with baking paper. Pour mixture into tin. Break woody ends from washed asparagus. Trim asparagus to even lengths and arrange over muffin mixture. Scrunch up prosciutto and arrange over asparagus. Bake at 180°C for 20 minutes or until muffin mixture springs back when lightly touched. Serve hot with hollandaise sauce.

COOK'S TIP

If you want to make hollandaise sauce ahead of time and worry about it splitting, keep it warm in a thermos flask.

small cakes

There's always something quite refined about serving small cakes for morning or afternoon tea, in a packed lunch or for a magnificent dessert.

Look out for interesting cake tins to make your small cake baking even more chic.

Fancy shaped tins, paper cases and even individual wooden crates make small cake baking a creative experience for every cook.

Honey and Almond Friands
Makes 6. See photograph on pages 46–47.

100g butter

1/4 cup honey

4 egg whites

1 cup plain flour

1/2 cup icing sugar

Melt butter and honey in a saucepan, heating until it starts to bubble. Remove from heat. Beat egg whites until lightly frothy in a bowl large enough to mix all the ingredients. Sift flour and icing sugar into egg whites. Add butter mixture and fold until flour and butter mixtures are combined with egg whites. Three-quarters fill greased friand or deep muffin pans with mixture. Spoon over topping. Bake at 180°C for 15–20 minutes or until cakes spring back when lightly touched.

TOPPING

25g butter

1/4 cup honey

70g packet slivered almonds

TOPPING

Melt butter, honey and almonds in a saucepan until boiling. Remove from heat.

Very Lemon Cakes
Makes 6. See photograph on page 49.

150g softened butter

1/2 cup sugar

1 cup lemon curd

1 teaspoon grated lemon rind

3 eggs

1 cup plain flour

3 teaspoons baking powder

1/2 cup custard powder

1/2 cup sugar cubes

1/4 cup lemon juice

Beat butter, sugar, lemon curd and lemon rind together with a wooden spoon until combined. Beat eggs and mix into butter mixture. Sift in flour, baking powder and custard powder and mix to combine. Half fill greased jumbo muffin pans or fancy cake tins with the mixture. Lightly crush sugar cubes and sprinkle over cakes. Bake at 180°C for 30–35 minutes or until cakes spring back when lightly touched. Pour lemon juice over cakes and bake a further 5 minutes. Cool in tin for 10 minutes before removing.

COOK'S TIP
You can make your own lemon curd if wished. Here's a simple recipe.

6 egg yolks

1 cup sugar

grated rind and juice of 4 lemons

100g butter

Mix egg yolks and sugar together in the top of a double boiler or in a bowl over simmering water. Stir mixture until it thickens and coats the back of a wooden spoon. Mix in the lemon rind and juice. Cut butter into cubes. Gradually add the butter to the lemon mixture, whisking after each addition. Pour mixture into hot, clean, dry jars. Seal when cold and store in the refrigerator.

Makes about 2½ cups.

Raspberry Shortbread Cakes Makes 8.

150g butter
1 teaspoon vanilla essence
$^1/_2$ cup icing sugar
$^1/_2$ cup cornflour
$^3/_4$ cup plain flour
4 teaspoons raspberry jam
8 frozen raspberries
icing sugar (optional)

Melt butter in a saucepan large enough to mix all the ingredients. Remove from heat and mix in vanilla essence. Sift in icing sugar, cornflour and flour and mix until combined. Fill greased patty pans with mixture. Make a dent in the top of the mixture with your thumb. Place $^1/_2$ teaspoon of raspberry jam in the dent. Top with a frozen raspberry. Bake at 160°C for 45 minutes or until cooked. Dust with icing sugar if desired.

Chocolate Apple Cakes Makes 8.

150g butter

³/₄ cup sugar

3 eggs

2 cups plain flour

¹/₄ cup cocoa

3 teaspoons baking powder

567g can apple slices

icing sugar

Melt butter in a saucepan large enough to mix all the ingredients. Remove from heat and mix in sugar and eggs until combined. Sift flour, cocoa and baking powder into mixture. Beat with a wooden spoon until smooth. Half fill eight 6 x 5cm deep paper cases with mixture. Top with apple slices then with chocolate mixture to fill the cases. Bake at 180°C for 15–20 minutes or until firm and cooked. Dust with icing sugar to serve.

Auntie Minnie's Orange Arfty Cakes Makes 45.

Afternoon tea served from the tea trolley in china crockery always featured a plain version of these cakes. Here's mine.

5 sheets flaky pastry

1^1/$_4$ cups plum jam

125g butter

1 cup sugar

2 eggs

^{3}/$_4$ cup orange Juice

1 teaspoon grated orange rind

2 cups plain flour

4 teaspoons baking powder

Cut 45 x 7cm rounds from pastry sheets and use to line patty pans. Place a teaspoon of jam in the bottom of each pastry shell. Melt butter in a saucepan large enough to mix all the ingredients. Mix in sugar. Remove from heat and beat in eggs, orange juice and rind using a wire whisk. Sift in flour and baking powder and mix with a wooden spoon to combine. Three-quarters fill pastry cases with mixture. Bake at 200°C for 15 minutes or until golden and cakes spring back when lightly touched.

Tim's Gingerbread Cakes Makes 7.

150g butter

1 cup golden syrup

^{3}/$_4$ cup brown sugar

1 cup ginger beer

2 teaspoons baking soda

2^1/$_2$ cups plain flour

1 tablespoon ground ginger

2 teaspoons mixed spice

Melt butter, golden syrup and brown sugar in a saucepan large enough to mix all the ingredients. Remove from heat and add ginger beer and baking soda. While the mixture is frothing, mix in sifted flour, ginger and mixed spice until mixture is smooth. Line the base of seven 9 x 6cm tins or friand tins. Pour mixture into the tins. Bake at 180°C for 35 minutes or until cakes spring back when lightly touched. Serve with butter or ginger marmalade if desired.

COOK'S TIP

Vary the flavour of Auntie Minnie's Orange Arfty Cakes for a change. Replace the orange juice with milk and the orange rind with a teaspoon of almond essence. Raspberry jam works well with almond flavours so use this instead of plum jam.

Cappuccino Friands Makes 5.

100g butter

4 egg whites

$^3/_4$ cup plain flour

$^1/_4$ cup very finely ground espresso coffee beans

1 cup icing sugar

$^1/_2$ teaspoon mixed spice

TOPPING

1 egg white

$^1/_4$ cup sugar

Heat butter in a saucepan until it turns golden. Remove from heat. Beat egg whites until soft peaks form. Fold flour, coffee and icing sugar into egg whites. Pour butter into mixture and fold to combine. Half fill greased friand tins with mixture. Spoon over topping and sprinkle with mixed spice. Bake at 180°C for 15–20 minutes or until friands are cooked and meringue lightly golden.

TOPPING

Beat egg white until frothy. Beat in sugar until thick and glossy.

Quick Individual New York Style Cheesecakes Makes 14.

Serve these for dessert or afternoon tea.

8 digestive biscuits

¼ cup sugar

50g butter

CHEESECAKE

500g cream cheese

1 cup lemon curd

3 eggs

Crush biscuits to fine crumbs in a food processor or blender or by crushing in a plastic bag. Mix in sugar. Melt butter and mix into crumbs. Line the base of deep patty pans. Press 2 tablespoons of mixture into each pan. Pour in cheesecake mixture. Bake at 150°C for 25–30 minutes or until set. Serve at room temperature.

CHEESECAKE

Soften cream cheese to packet directions. Place cream cheese, lemon curd and eggs in the bowl of a food processor. Process until combined.

COOK'S TIP

You can make your own lemon curd if desired. See the recipe on page 48.

Little Dream-Date Cakes Makes 16. See photograph on page 57.

125g butter

$1/2$ cup brown sugar

$1^1/_2$ cups plain flour

$1^1/_2$ teaspoons baking powder

16 dates

TOPPING

2 eggs

1 cup brown sugar

2 tablespoons cornflour

$1/2$ teaspoon baking powder

2 cups coconut

$1/2$ cup finely chopped walnuts

Heat butter and brown sugar in a saucepan until butter melts. Remove from heat. Sift in flour and baking powder and mix until combined. Press $1^1/4$ tablespoons of mixture into the base of greased patty pans. Bake at 190°C for 10 minutes. Remove from oven and place a date on each base. Pour topping over base to three-quarters fill greased patty pans or fancy cake tins. Bake at 160°C for 15–20 minutes or until golden and set. Cool in tin for 10 minutes before removing.

TOPPING

Beat eggs and brown sugar together until thick. Sift cornflour and baking powder into egg mixture and mix in with coconut and walnuts until combined. Serve with freshly whipped cream.

Semolina Orange Dessert Cake Serves 8. (Not photographed.)

If, preferred, this cake can be cooked in a baking paper, bottom lined 20cm cake tin. Bake at 180°C for 45 minutes.

2 oranges

125g low-fat butter

$3/4$ cup sugar

2 eggs

2 cups semolina

1 tablespoon baking powder

Place oranges in a saucepan and cover with water. Bring to the boil and simmer for about 20 minutes or until oranges are soft. Drain, cool and cut into chunks, discarding pips. Place oranges, butter, sugar and eggs in the bowl of a food processor and process until oranges are chopped and mixture combined. Mix semolina and baking powder together and add to processor. Process until just combined. Pour mixture into deep paper cases. Bake at 180°C for 20–25 minutes or until cake springs back when lightly touched.

Pina Colada Cakes Makes 12.

I like cakes that are versatile. These can be served for dessert or wrapped for a lunch box.

440g can unsweetened crushed pineapple

150g softened butter

1 cup sugar

2 eggs

$1^1/_2$ cups plain flour

150g packet coconut milk powder mix

1 teaspoon baking soda

paper cases

Drain pineapple, reserving juice. Place butter, sugar, eggs and pineapple in a mixer bowl. Mix on low speed until combined. Sift in flour, coconut milk powder and baking soda. Beat on low speed until combined. Stir in $^1/_2$ cup reserved pineapple juice. Increase speed to medium and beat for 2 minutes. Place paper cases in patty pans. Three-quarters fill cases with mixture. Bake at 180°C for 25–30 minutes or until lightly golden and cakes spring back when lightly touched. Serve warm as a dessert with grilled pineapple and ice cream or as cakes.

Notre Dame Cakes Makes 4.

500g mixed glacé fruits
150g blanched almonds
100g shelled pistachio nuts
4 eggs
³/₄ cup caster sugar
¹/₂ cup orange-flavoured liqueur
1 cup plain flour
1 teaspoon baking powder
1 teaspoon mixed spice
icing sugar

Chop glacé fruit if necessary. Mix fruit, almonds and pistachio nuts together. Beat the eggs, sugar and liqueur together in a bowl large enough to mix all the ingredients. Sift flour, baking powder and mixed spice into bowl and fold into egg mixture. Add fruit and nut mixture and fold in. Line the base of 13 x 10cm mini loaf tins with baking paper. Three-quarters fill the the tins with mixture. Bake at 160°C for 35–40 minutes or until an inserted skewer comes out clean. Cool in tins before removing. Serve dusted with icing sugar.

Petite Pear and Ginger Fruit Cakes Makes 5.

This mixture makes a great Christmas cake. It can be cooked in a 20cm round cake tin with newspaper tied around the outside edge of the tin and the tin sitting on layers of newspaper in the oven as described below. Bake at 150°C for 1½ hours. Lower temperature to 130°C and cook for a further 2–2½ hours or until an inserted skewer comes out clean.

500g dried pears

250g crystallised ginger

250g raisins

½ cup plain flour

250g butter

1½ cups dark cane sugar

2 tablespoons treacle

4 eggs

1 tablespoon grated lemon rind

1 teaspoon vanilla essence

1 teaspoon ground ginger

1 teaspoon ground cardamom

1¾ cups plain flour

¼ teaspoon baking soda

1 cup blanched almonds

5 tablespoons brandy

Roughly chop pears and ginger. Place in a bowl with raisins and toss through first measure of sifted flour. Melt butter in a saucepan large enough to mix all the ingredients. Mix in sugar and treacle. Remove from heat, cool if necessary. Beat in eggs with a wooden spoon. Mix in lemon rind and vanilla. Sift ginger, cardamom, second measure of flour and baking soda into mixture and stir to combine with fruit mixture. Line the base of five 10cm round cake tins with baking paper. Divide the mixture evenly among tins. Decorate with almonds. Tie or use sticky tape to secure four layers of newspaper around the outside edge of the cake tins so the newspaper stands about 3cm above the top of the tin. Place six layers of newspaper on the shelf in a 160°C oven. Place cake tins on this. Bake cakes for 40 minutes. Lower temperature to 150°C and bake a further 30 minutes or until an inserted skewer comes out clean. Remove from oven and pour one tablespoon of brandy over the surface of each cake. Cool in tin before removing.

COOK'S TIP

These pear and ginger fruit cakes were almost mass-produced in my kitchen last Christmas. You can use any combination of fruit you like, replacing the pears, crystallised ginger and raisins with 1kg of any other fruit combination.

Black Rice and Coconut Dessert Cakes Makes 14.

These are not stunning to look at but they taste divine.

1 cup black sticky rice

3 cups coconut cream

4 egg whites

$^1/_2$ cup sugar

$^1/_2$ cup desiccated coconut

$^1/_2$ cup rice flour

Place black sticky rice and coconut cream in a saucepan and cook over a moderate heat for 40 minutes, stirring occasionally, or until cooked. Cool. Beat egg whites until frothy. Beat in sugar until thick and glossy. Fold coconut and rice flour into egg whites. Mix cooked rice into egg-white mixture. Three-quarters fill greased deep patty pans with mixture. Bake at 180°C for 30 minutes or until firm. Stand for 10 minutes before turning out. Serve warm or cold with coconut ice cream and fresh tropical fruit. Store in the refrigerator.

Summer Pudding Trifle Cakes Makes 10.

4 cups mixed berries such as raspberries, blackberries and strawberries

$^1/_2$ cup sugar

20cm trifle sponge

$^1/_2$ cup whipped cream

1 cup custard

Prepare fruit as necessary. Mix fruit and sugar together in a saucepan and heat until almost boiling. Cool. Cut sponge into 2cm cubes. Pack half of the sponge pieces into the bottom of 10 deep paper cases set in deep patty pans. Spoon over berry mixture. Top with more sponge pieces, pressing down. Cover patty pans with plastic wrap. Place a board on top and refrigerate for two hours or overnight. When ready to serve, remove wrap. Invert patty pan onto a board. Place trifle cakes on a serving plate. Mix cream and custard together and serve with cakes.

index

savoury muffins

Apple and Sausage Muffins	16
Carrot and Coriander Muffins	15
Cheese Muffins	11
Dill and Horseradish Muffins with	
Smoked Salmon	8
French Onion Muffins	16
Fresh Herb Muffins	8
Lemon and Thyme Muffins	8
Minted Pea Muffins	10
Moroccan Muffins	19
Olive and Feta Muffins	16
Roasted Capsicum Muffins	12
Thai Muffins	18
Tomato and Chorizo Muffins	14
Walnut and Blue Cheese Muffins	12

sweet muffins

Apple Dumpling Muffins	32
Bran and Sticky Raisin Muffins	24
Bread and Butter Muffins	31
Carrot and Honey Muffins	22
Cherry Muffins	28
Chocolate Brownie Muffins	
with Mixed Berry Sauce	22
Chocolate Spice Muffins	27
Crushed Berry and White Chocolate Muffins	32
Date and Marsala Muffins	26
Honey and Hazelnut Muffins	29
Peach Melba Muffins	30
Prune and Orange Muffins	22
Raspberry and Rhubarb Muffins	25
Rhubarb and Lemon Muffins	32

muffin mixtures

Apple Strudel Muffin Dessert	43
Asparagus Slice with	
Crisp Prosciutto and Hollandaise Sauce	44
Beetroot, Feta and Pistachio Muffin Slice	36
Breakfast Egg Muffins	36
Curried Chicken Muffin Bake	38
Magic Muffins	40
Muffin-Topped Chilli Con Carne	44
Quince Paste, Blue Cheese and Walnut Fingers	42
Rosemary and Onion-Jam Muffin Loaf	39

small cakes

Auntie Minnie's Orange Arfty Cakes	53
Black Rice and Coconut Dessert Cakes	62
Cappuccino Friands	54
Chocolate Apple Cakes	51
Honey and Almond Friands	48
Little Dream-Date Cakes	56
Notre Dame Cakes	59
Petite Pear and Ginger Fruit Cakes	60
Pina Colada Cakes	58
Quick Individual New York Style Cheesecakes	55
Raspberry Shortbread Cakes	50
Semolina Orange Dessert Cake	56
Summer Pudding Trifle Cakes	63
Tim's Gingerbread Cakes	53
Very Lemon Cakes	48